THE BIG STORM 1952

Edited by
C. L. Neely

The Big Storm
1952

ISBN: 9798324730611

Copyright © 2024 by C. L. Neely
All rights reserved.

No part of this publication can be reproduced or transmitted in any form or by any means electronic or mechanical (beyond that copying permitted by U. S. Copyright Law, Section 107, "fair use" in teaching or research. Section 108, certain library copying, or in publishing media by reviewers in limited excerpt), without permission in writing from C. L. Neely.

                    carrien2u@yahoo.com

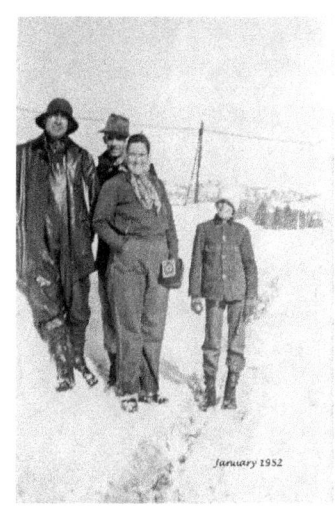
January 1952

In Memory of Bertha Miller

Pictured in the center of this photo is Bertha Miller holding an old box camera. For those who are not familiar with a box camera, they were a small camera shaped like a box. Often the lens was plastic and the photos came out blurry unless properly cared for.

Using this camera, in 1952, Bertha took many photos of the Big Storm, and they are included in this book. At that time she was a wife and mother and many of her pictures were of her house and family. It is unknown who took the photograph on this page. Her husband Jack is behind her and son Dennis is to her left. The man in the rain coat is unknown.

Later Bertha went on to become a photographer and news correspondent for the Reno Evening Gazette and Sacramento Bee. Her articles and photos can be found in several books by this author, ranging from 1955 to 1961.

The Big Storm

(Note: The newspaper articles found in this book were not written by Bertha Miller. She did not begin writing for newspapers until a couple of years later.)

Christmas 1951

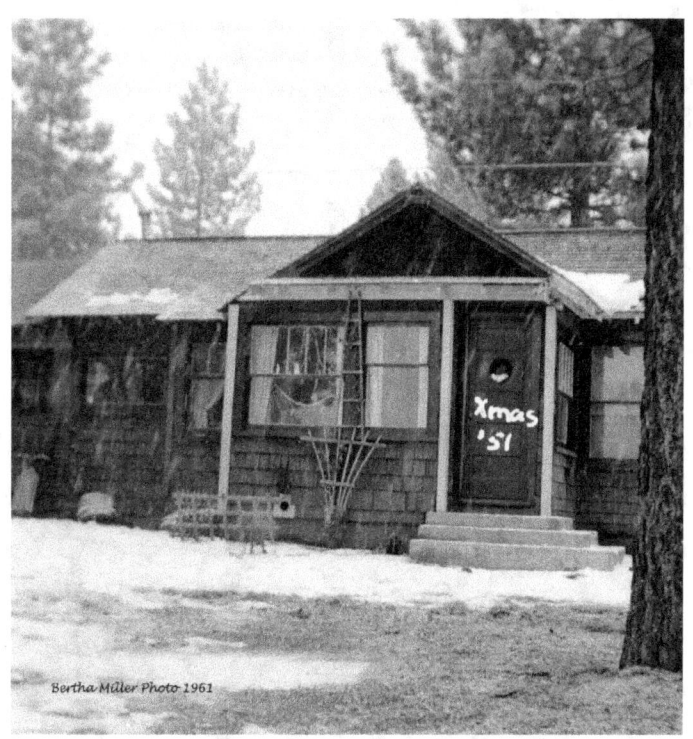

Bertha Miller Photo 1961

In 1951 the Miller family resided in the Sierra Nevada Mountains, in the small town of Portola. They lived in a cute little house on Ridge Street that they referred to as Grandpa Rice's house. It was tiny, to say the least, but a move forward from the apartment they lived in before this.

Like in other families the children looked forward to winter snow and all the activities that came with it. They never expected the BIG STORM that came only a few weeks later.

Christmas 1951

Enough snow to enjoy the new sled and build a snowman.

Carrie Miller and Pepper

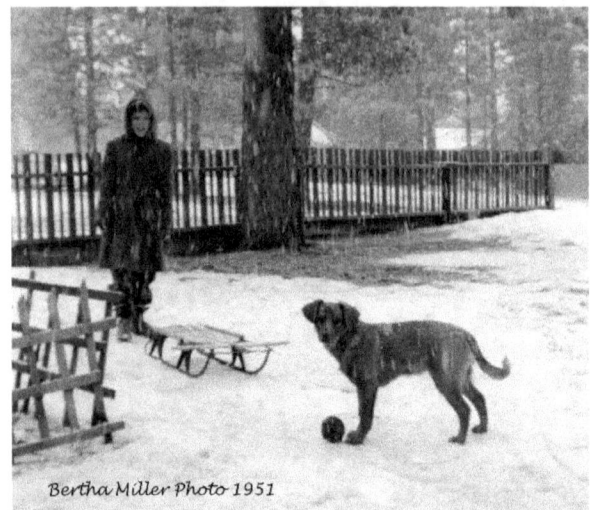

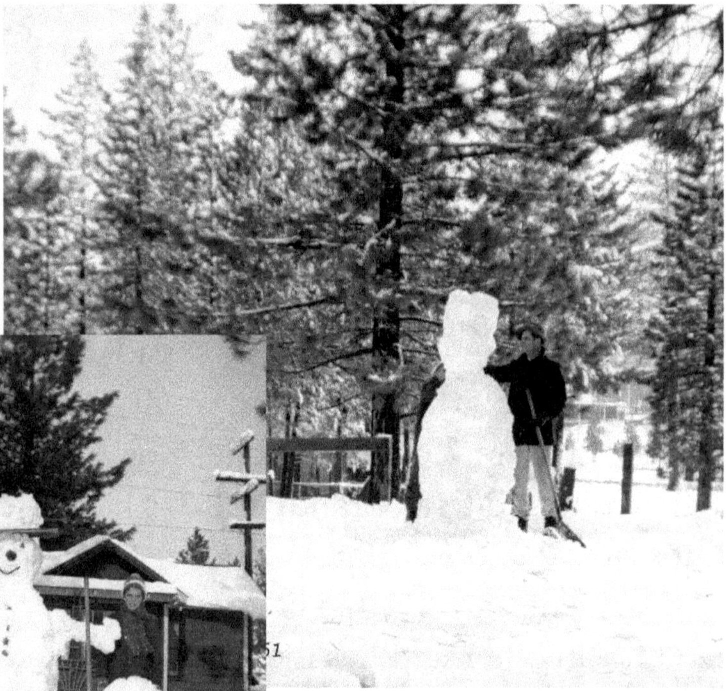

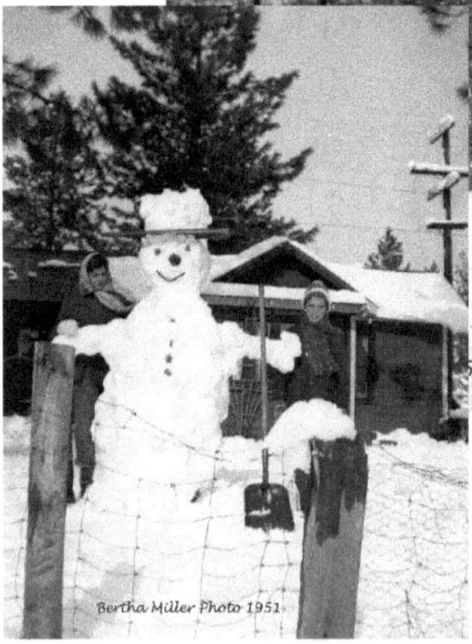

Above: Jack & Dennis Miller

Finished snowman Kathy & Dennis Miller

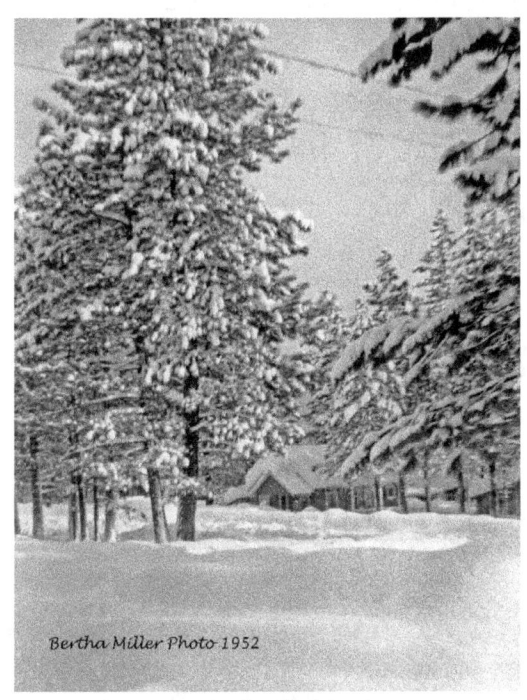
Bertha Miller Photo 1952

BIG STORM
Portola Reporter ~ January 17, 1952

A state of threatened disaster was proclaimed in Portola Wednesday afternoon as the city and the entire area grappled with the effects of the worst snow storm in their history, with a brief respite of sunlight and a threat of another storm coming in.

The proclamation was issued by Rex Reihm, disaster council commander, under a city ordinance, and was approved by Mayor George M. Saxton. It was issued on recommendation of the governor's office and state disaster council officials.

Governor Warren, Wednesday morning, ordered all state agencies to assist in relieving the local conditions in every way possible.

The action followed a conference of the disaster council, city officials and others in the justice court, at which an appraisal of the situation was taken.

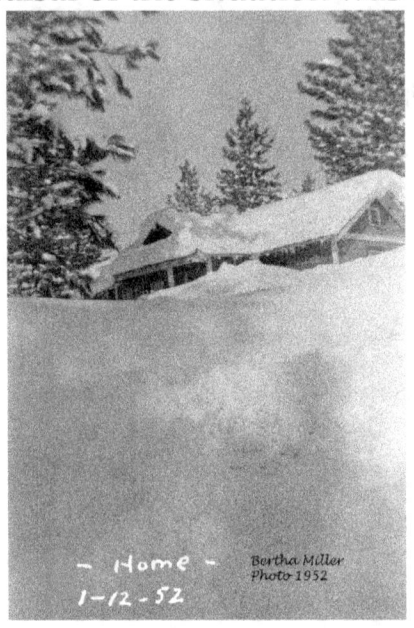
— Home —
1-12-52
Bertha Miller
Photo 1952

Reihm declared the situation is getting more critical and another storm was forecast. The supply situation is not bad yet, but it is getting worse, he declared, and added that four buildings had been lost, due to the weight of the snow.

"We've got to get the streets opened up," he added, citing that the fire department is practically immobile.

First problem, he said, was snow removal from houses and commercial buildings, and the second was opening of streets.

He reported he had contacted Dale C. Williams,

regional defense coordinator in Redding, who was calling Sacramento for assistance. Williams also contacted the Herlong munitions base for supplies and equipment, but Commander Howard, of Herlong, later advised Reihm that the base is in need of emergency equipment.

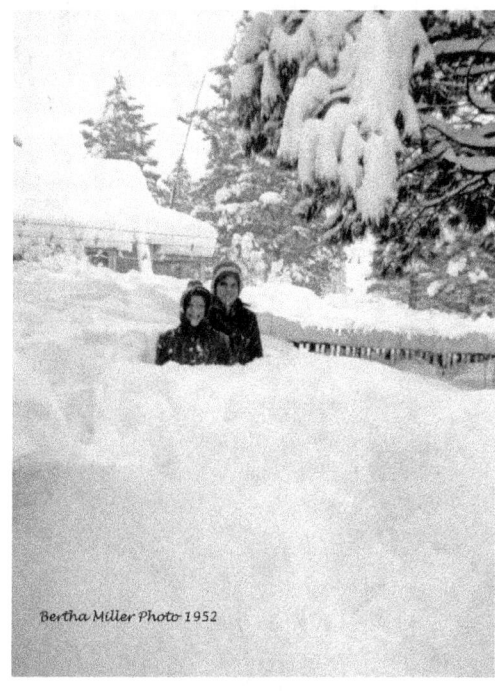

Carrie and Dennis Miller

Mayor Saxton and Supervisor Clair Donnenwirth declared that the situation was beyond the ability of the city and council.

They were asked to coordinate their efforts, with a view of determining what additional steps could be taken. Donnenwirth has been directing snow removal on Commercial Street and county roads for days.

Ralph Cullen was asked to check the stores as to supplies and later reported absence of fresh meat, yeast for bread, milk and shortages of other foods.

Councilman John Richards reported fuel oil supplies running low, with all distributors pooling their supplies and equipment to make distributions.

Saxton reported that the Western Pacific has offered the city equipment available to help the city.

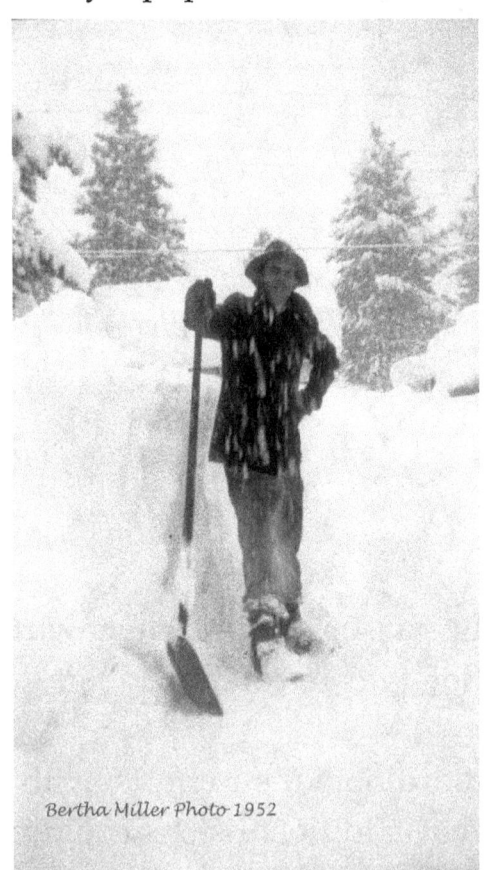

Jack Miller

Bertha Miller Photo 1952

Ed Groves and O. E. Rooney were placed in charge

of snow removal from roofs and asked to recruit shovelers.

Dr. R. M. Peters reported a shortage of drugs, particularly penicillin, at the hospital, and arrangements were made through the disaster council either to fly in a supply from Sacramento and drop them on the ball park or ship them from

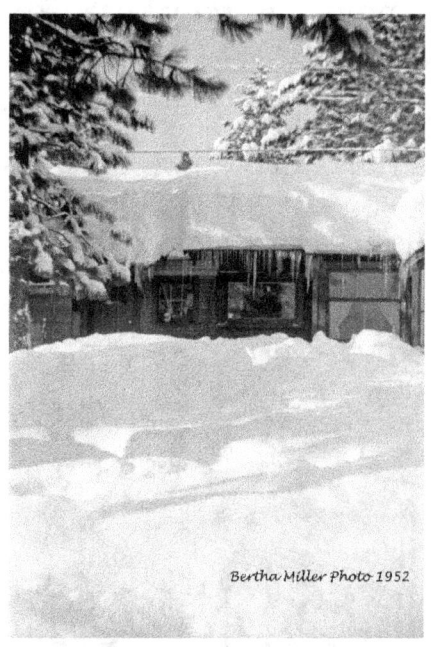

Bertha Miller Photo 1952

Herlong. The latter plan was adopted.

L. C. DeArmond, owner of the Portola Water Company, announced that in the event of a power failure, restriction on the use of water would be necessary, and urged minimum use. He said the Western Pacific is pumping water into city mains and relieving the situation.

Fire Chief James Johnson urged all citizens to

inspect chimneys and heating equipment, because the volunteer fire department is practically helpless.

Glenn Lee was placed in charge of distributing public appeals for cooperation.

Chief of Police Drew suggested that the ball park be cleared and cars that are stalled be towed there, so streets may be opened, declaring it is impossible on many streets to move the snow because of the cars.

Riehm ordered that clearing the ball park be made the first order of business.

And already the storm had taken heavy toll in Portola.

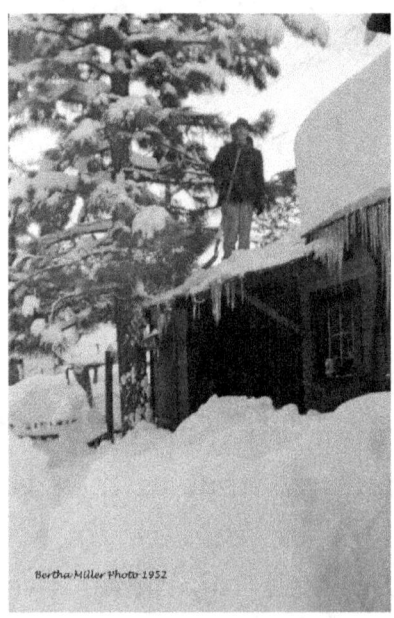

Bertha Miller Photo 1952

Sunday the unused Wonderland laundry building collapsed and Tuesday the weight of the snow caved in the Sterling Motel and threatened other cabins on the property which is owned by Earl Haynes.

Other buildings in the city were endangered, including the Freeman Fuel Company building, and scores of windows at the high school were broken by the snow.

The snow on the level in Portola was about seven feet, with huge drifts and piles of previously plowed snow mounting skyward.

Riehm expressed chief concern over the reportedly approaching storm.

M. F. Small, secretary to Governor Warren, called to advise the governor had instructed officials "to do everything necessary" to relieve the city and had instructed all state agencies to take all possible action.

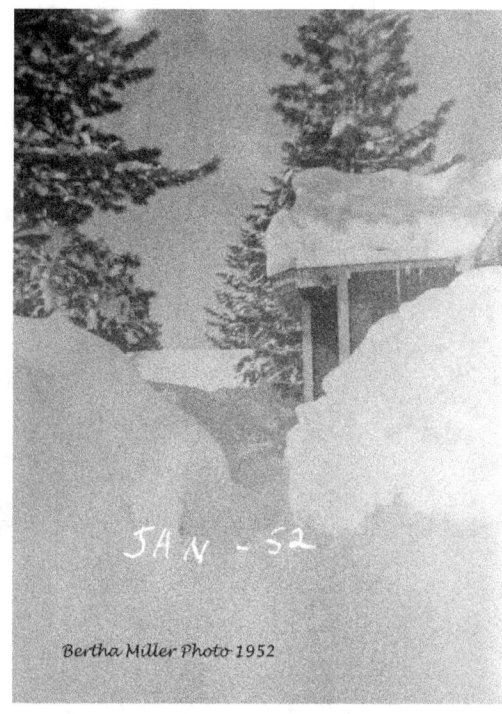

Bertha Miller Photo 1952

Calls from the state officials and from Rex Riehm to Herlong for equipment to be sent by the Western Pacific, brought the word from Col. Howard, commanding, that the base itself is badly in need of snow removal equipment.

The Western Pacific was open to the east, but no forecast could be made as to when the road through the canyon would be reopened, according to Virgil Edwards, trainmaster. He reported that Sunday a snow plow took nine hours to go the nine miles to Clio and had to turn back for lack of water. Edwards said that the effort to drive a snowplow through to Reno, would be made by snowplow today (Thursday).

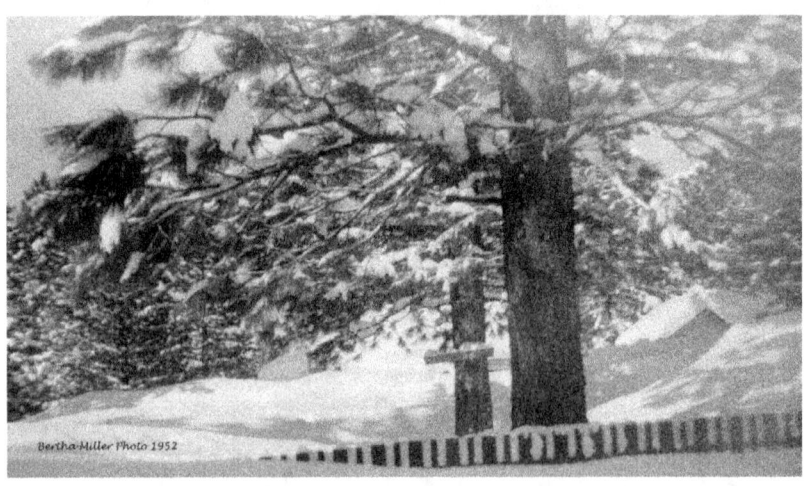

Bertha Miller Photo 1952

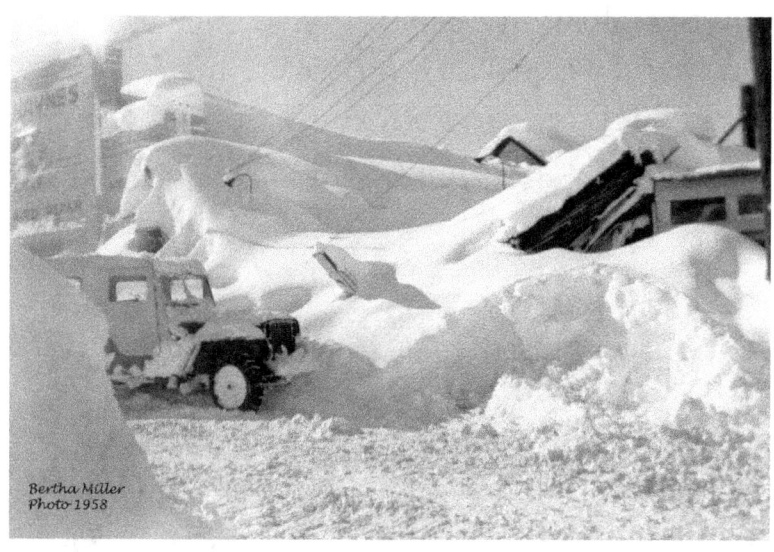

Bertha Miller Photo 1958

Buildings Collapse Under Snow
Portola Reporter ~ January 17, 1952

Weight of the snow took a heavy toll of Portola buildings during the storm.

The Sterling Motel, owned by Earl Haynes, collapsed Tuesday afternoon and six cabins at the motel were in danger.

The Wonderland laundry building, long unused, also crashed to the ground early Sunday. L. C. DeArmond was standing directly in front of the building and jumped to safety as flying glass sprayed out onto the street.

A warehouse building of James Johnson also collapsed and it was thought the force of the English home explosion might have been the trigger that caused the fall.

Frantic and successful efforts were made to save the Freeman Fuel company office.

Various other buildings in the city also were in danger.

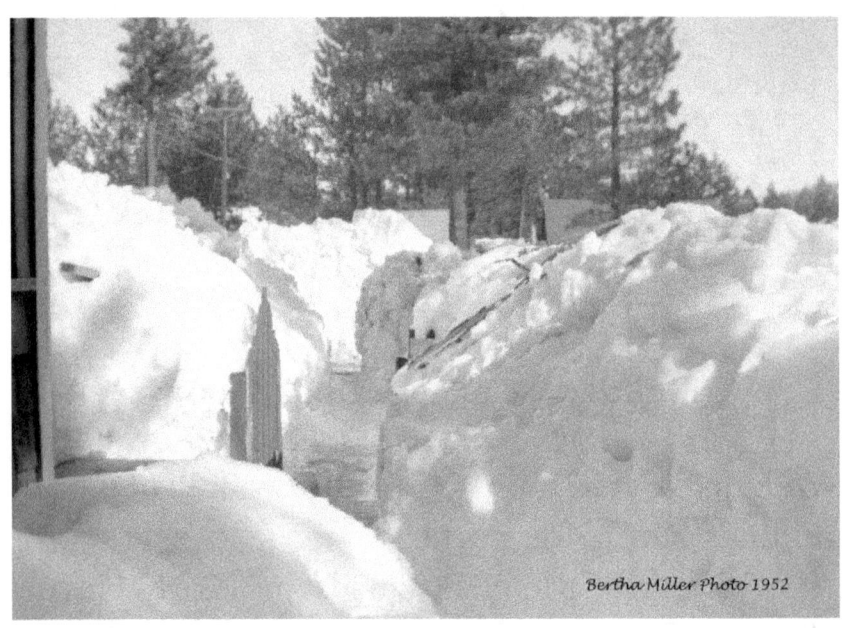

Bertha Miller Photo 1952

Explosion
Portola Reporter ~ January 17, 1952

As a dramatic climax of the worst storm in Portola's history, Mrs Gertrude English, 21, was killed outright in an explosion that wrecked their home at 3:50 a.m. Wednesday morning. Her husband, Robert, suffered "moderately severe" cuts and bruises.

The blast, presumably from a gas or oil stove, shook houses for blocks around, severely damaged the adjacent home of Bert English and broke windows in other homes.

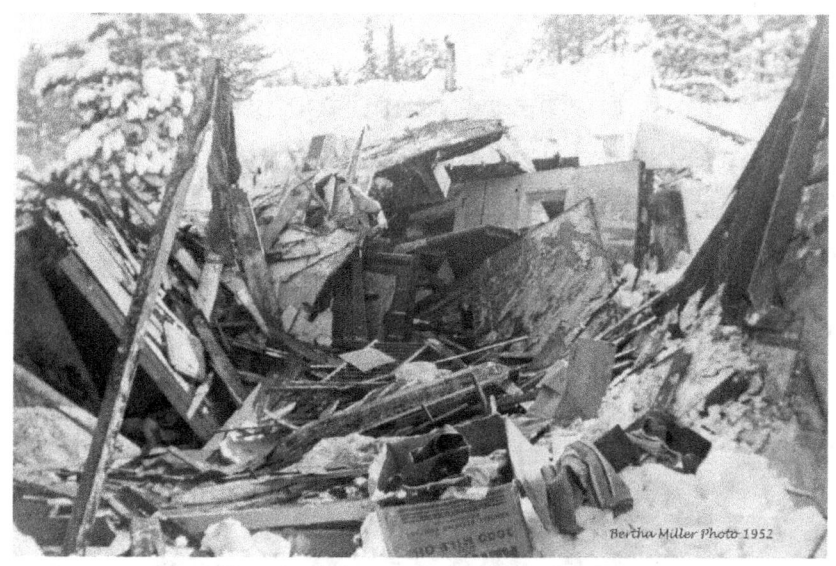

English home after explosion.

The Portola volunteer fire department, battled through huge drifts for nearly one half hour to reach the scene a short distance away. A bulldozer with a snow plow broke the way for the fire engine, and the body and the injured man were taken out by truck.

Frantically the snow plow lunged and clawed at great drifts, lighted by the eerie flames of the still burning gas escaping from the tank, while firemen and Western Pacific employees battled to get to the trapped people. The English daughter was visiting her grandmother in Reno at the time.

Mrs. English was the step sister of Don Caldwell and English is the son of Bert English. Mrs. English's mother resides in Miami, Fla.

While Caldwell was looking among the ruins of the demolished home, hours after the explosion, he heard the whimpering of a dog.

Digging into the debris found the English dog, hair singed and buried in the wreckage.

The mother of Robert English planned to fly to Portola by ski plane from Reno yesterday afternoon.

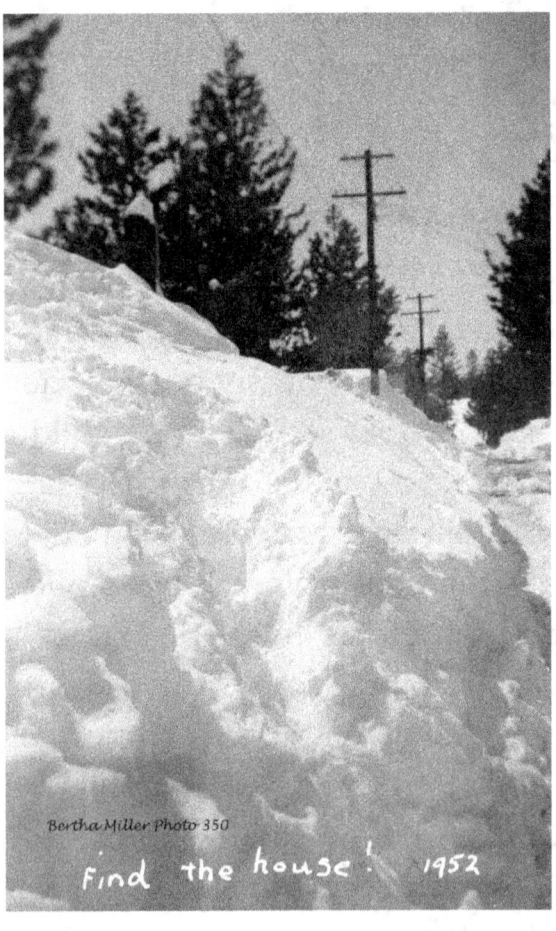

Bertha Miller Photo 350
Find the house! 1952

Fuel Dealers Pool Their Resources
Portola Reporter ~ January 17, 1952

Fuel oil and bottled gas dealers pooled their supplies and efforts Tuesday to keep householders and business houses supplied.

The combined headquarters of all distributors was established at the office of the Freeman Fuel Company, and snow plows assisted in making deliveries, it was announced by Supervisor Donnenwirth.

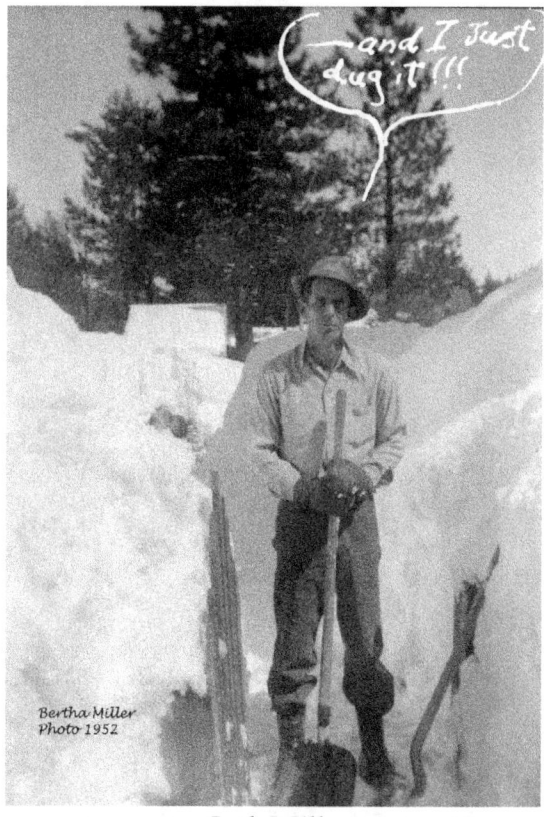

Jack Miller

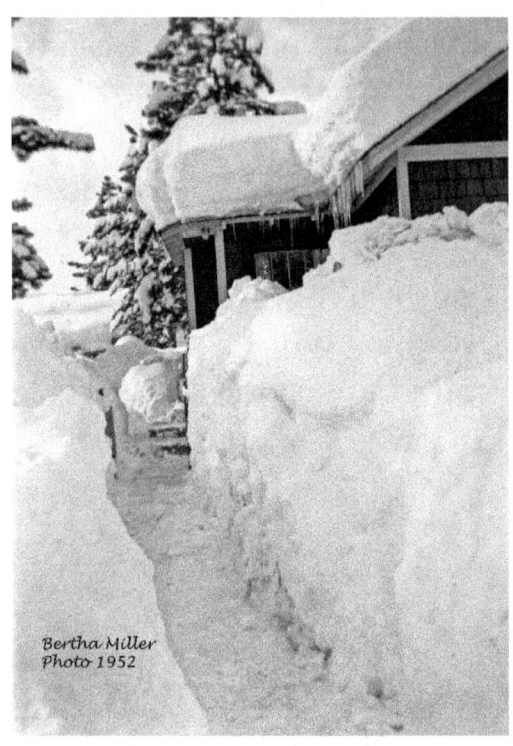
Bertha Miller
Photo 1952

Water Shortage Threatened in City
Portola Reporter ~ January 17, 1952

A water shortage threatened Portola during the heart of the big storm.

Failing power stopped the Portola Water company pumps and caused one of them to burn out.

The result was a drained reservoir that left numerous houses without water for a time.

Tuesday, L. C. DeArmond, owner, announced that the Western Pacific had connected one of its wells with the city system and, in the absence of a sustained power failure; he believed the situation was solved.

Bus Passengers Marooned in City
Portola Reporter ~ January 17, 1952

Five Pacific Greyhound and two Burlington busses, routed over highway 24 after all routes across the mountains had been closed, were stalled in Portola, starting Sunday evening.

The busses carried 113 passengers, 80 adults and two children on the Greyhound and 31 persons on the Burlington.

The Burlington arranged for the care and feeding of those passengers, and the Greyhound Tuesday offered to take care of those who were destitute; many spent their nights in the H. M. & J. Club and in the busses.

Others were taken care of in private homes. Mrs. Amy Dewhirst, home service chairman of the Red Cross, took three soldiers into her home, all of whom were over due from leave from their camps, two persons were cared for by Mrs. Peggy Croning, two by Mr. and Mrs. Andrew Vegel, one by Mrs. Andrew Esterby, a family by Mrs. Earl Flightmaster and others by various families, Mrs. Dewhirst reported.

The Portolans were paying for the food of the stranded persons.

Tuesday arrangements were made for the American Red Cross to care for the stranded people who were unable to finance themselves and to reimburse those who had cared for them.

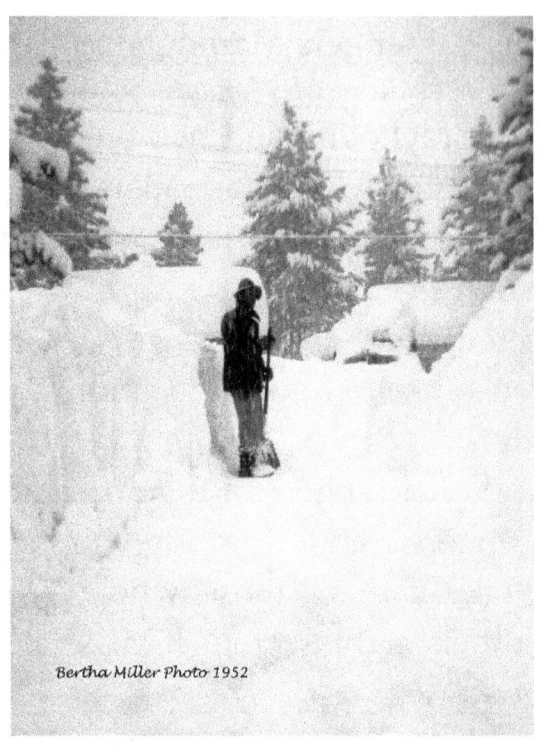
Bertha Miller Photo 1952

Emergency Ends
Portola Reporter ~ January 24, 1952

California's first civilian defense emergency of the basis of "threatened disaster' as a result of the Big Storm, was officially ended by order of Rex Riehm, commander, on Wednesday at 5 p.m.

Emergency traffic orders, restricting use of automobiles on the city streets to emergency travel by permit only, remain in effect it was announced by Chief of Police Drew.

In the meantime the city slowly dug out from beneath the worse storm in the city's history and one of the worst in the history of the state.

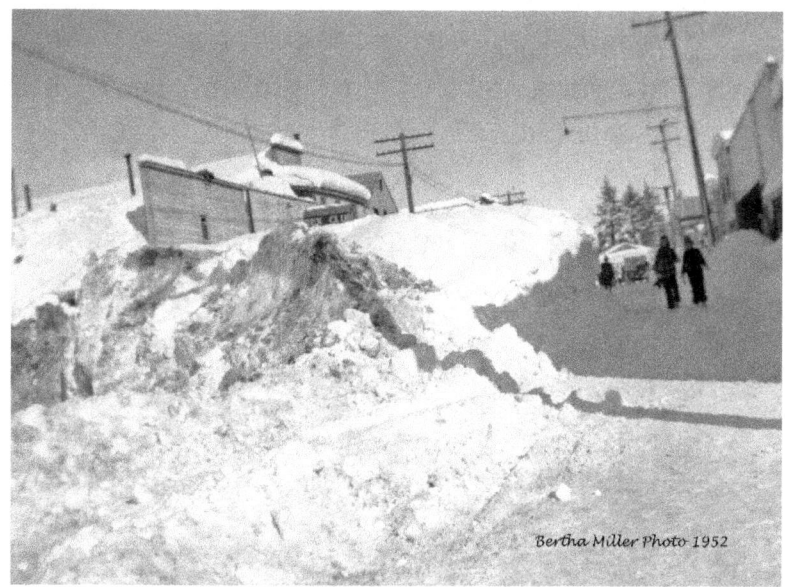

Commercial Street

One way traffic prevailed on many of the city streets with the snow piled many feed deep on the sides.

However, there remained threats of more snow or rain.

The San Francisco weather forecaster said there was a possibility of "fairly good rains," which could develop "into a serious situation" if it started to thaw the tremendous snow pack in the Sierra.

Highways in the area were beginning to be cleared. The road through Sierra Valley to Loyalton was reported in good shape Wednesday—at least for the time being.

The road to Hallelujah Junction was closed until Wednesday afternoon, and 395 was open to convoy traffic between Reno and Susanville.

Emergency traffic only was permitted on the highway between Portola and Quincy, and Quincy and Oroville.

A state of emergency in El Dorado County was declared Wednesday, in order to give assistance to the long suffering areas around Lake Tahoe.

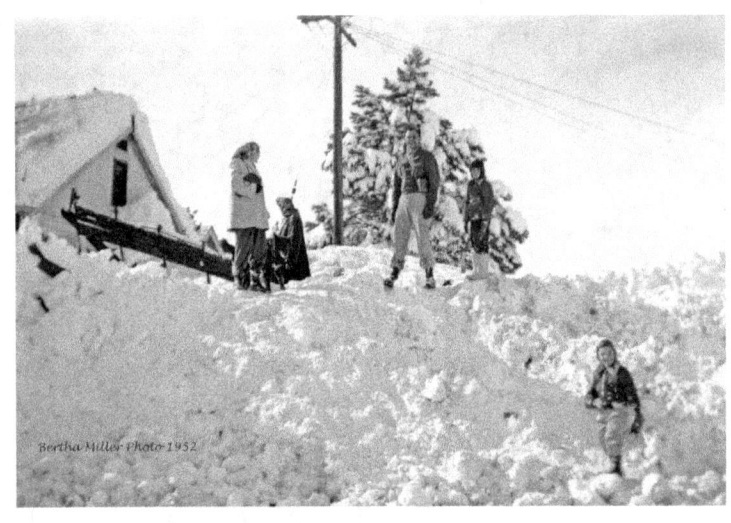

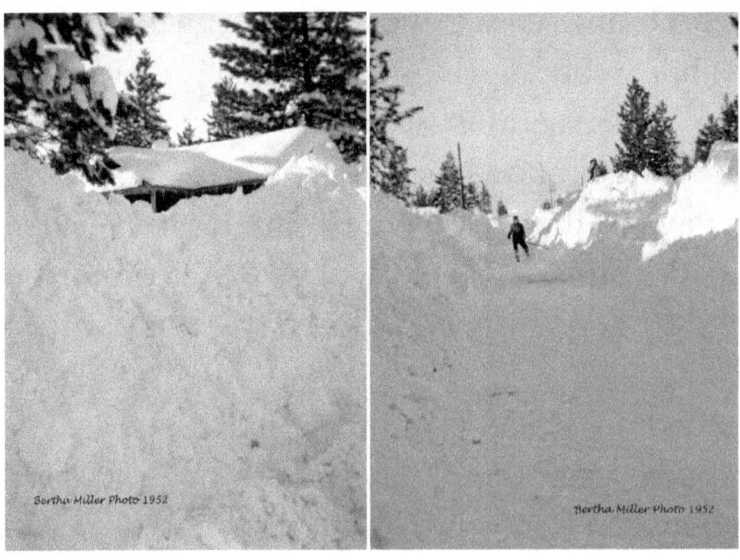

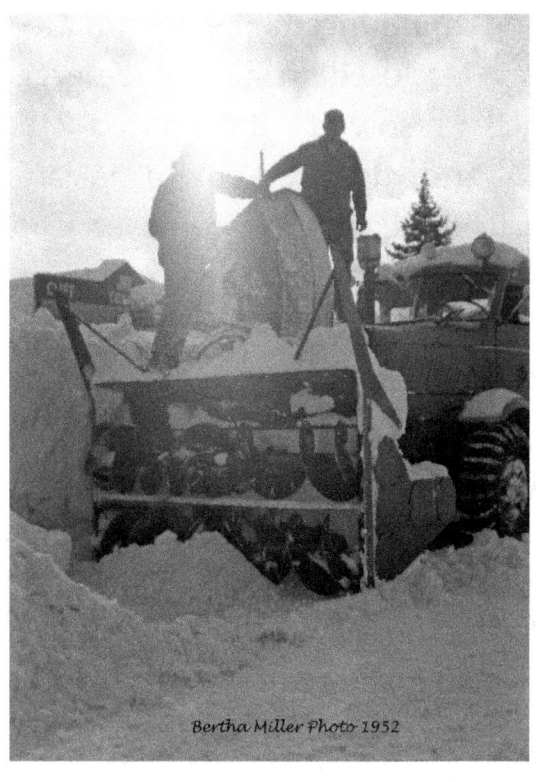

Bertha Miller Photo 1952

Portola Council Decries Report On Highway 24

Sacramento Bee ~ January 29, 1952

The Portola City Council last night adopted a resolution containing accusations that "false and misleading information" has been disseminated to the effect the Feather Route, Highway 24, is closed.

The resolution stated Highway 24 is open to two way traffic and has been for several days.

It recited the "false and misleading information" presumably was given out by state and unofficial agencies and announcements are made repeatedly the highway is closed to all but emergency traffic. The council resolved it decried the "untrue statements" and declared there is an "apparent conspiracy to mislead the people of California and Nevada into the belief there is no adequate highway communication between the states."

The resolution was directed to Governor Earl Warren and to the California Division of Highways.

Highway officials in Quincy, Plumas County, said conditions made Highway 24 unsafe for travel other than for emergency purposes. They declared the width of the road was only 14 feet and ice conditions where sand had not been completed made traveling hazardous.

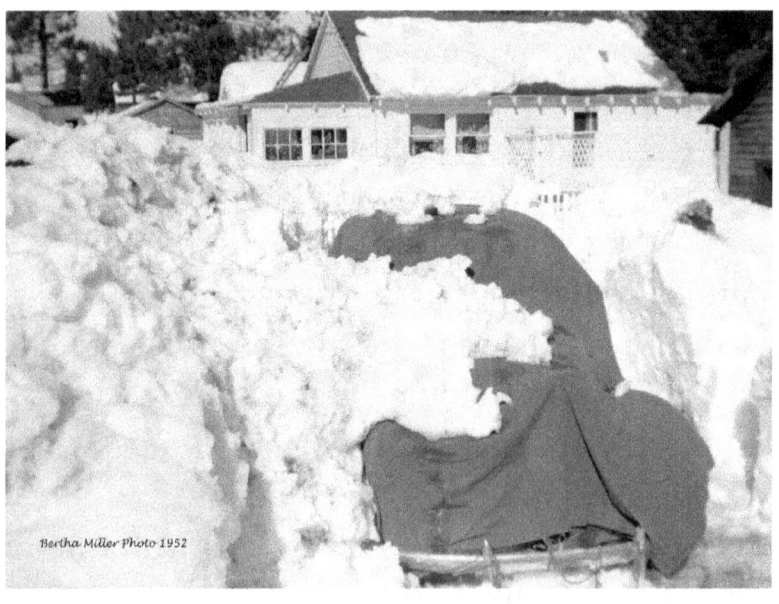

Bertha Miller Photo 1952

Feather River Road Ban is Criticized

Sacramento Bee ~ February 7, 1952

Stan Bailey, Portola editor, has asserted "there is a deliberate conspiracy to mislead the public about the condition of the Feather River Highway through the Sierra."

"I don't know who is responsible but the public is still told the road is open only for emergency travel when actually it has been bare to the pavement since Thursday," said Bailey, editor and chamber of commerce director.

The American Automobile Association at Reno listed the route today as open only to emergency and local travel between Blairsden and Hallelujah Junction.

The automobile association said it was told by the California Highway Department it does not want heavy traffic on the road because of high snow banks along each shoulder limiting the route to the two traffic lanes in that area.

But Bailey declared:

They tell us here the road is in such good shape that they've taken our plow for use elsewhere.

The highway could easily have accommodated those weekend tourists from the coast who wanted to go to the mountains or on into Reno.

Clarence Rowe showing depth of snow.

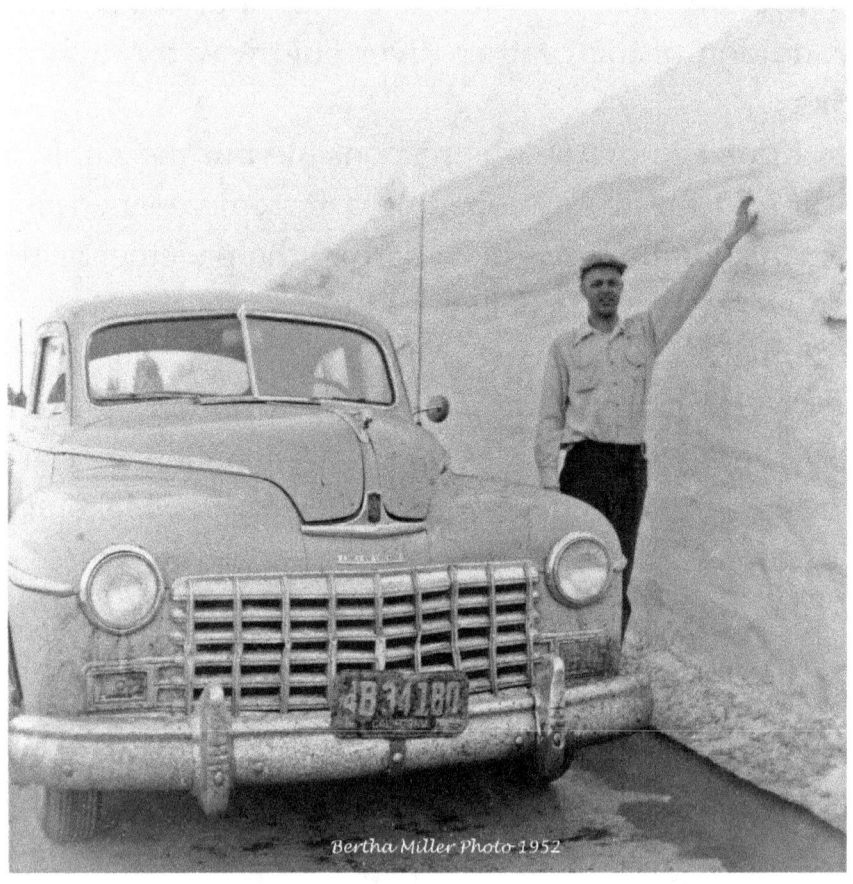

School Closed
Unknown source ~ January 24, 1952

Portola schools, closed Friday, January 11, when the Big Storm started, will open Monday, if weather and roads permit, it was announced by J. R. Daughenbaugh, high school principal.

The schools can't operate until two-way traffic is established for the busses, he said.

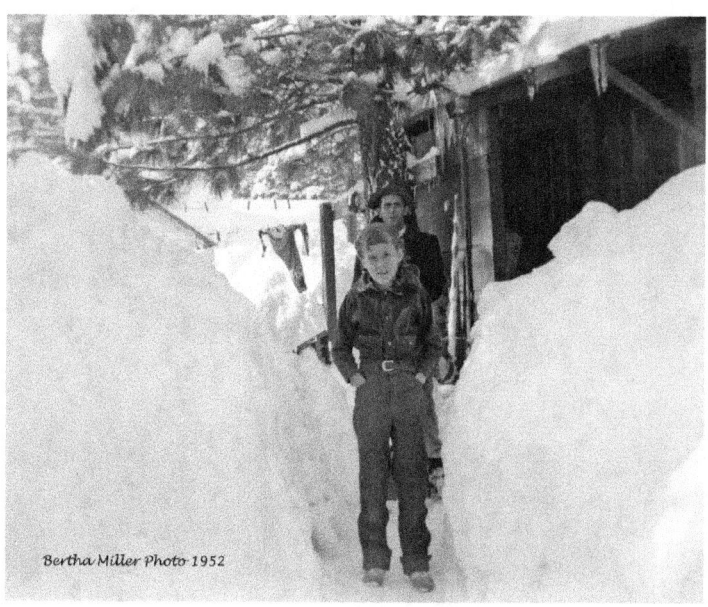

Happy to be home and playing in the snow!

School Girls Aid During Emergency
Unknown source ~ January 24, 1952

Portola high school girls, under direction of Glynn Lee, faculty member and member of the defense council, acted as Paul Reveres during the storm emergency last week.

A dozen girls, wading through deep drifts, distributed emergency instructions and orders throughout the community.

Rex Riehm, defense commander, paid a high tribute to the girls, saying they displayed the spirit of cooperation that typified the community during the battle with the storm.

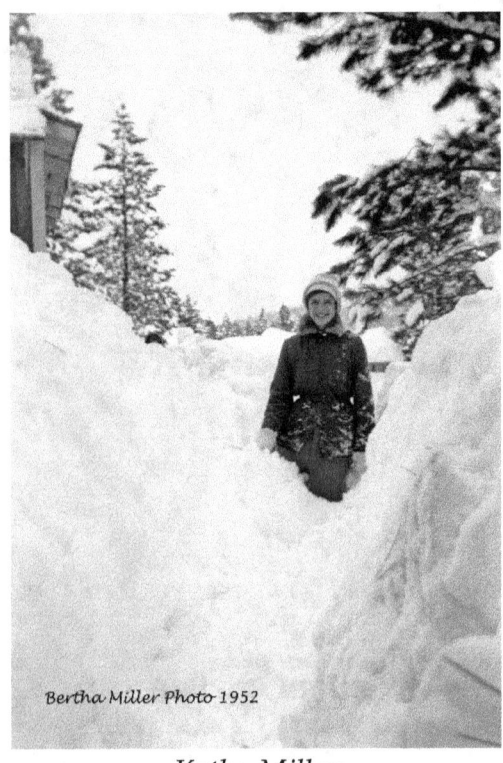

Kathy Miller

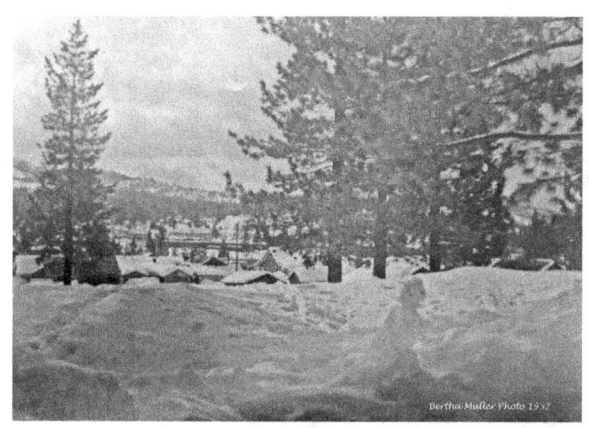
Bertha Muller Photo 1952

Storm Cost
Council, Defense Commander
View Situation in City
Portola Reporter ~ January 24, 1952

The cost of the Big Storm will amount to a terrific figure for the city of Portola, Rex Reihm, defense commander, told the city council at a meeting Monday night and will run into many thousands of dollars, according to Supervisor Clair Donnenwirth.

Later Reihm roughly estimated the cost of the storm, as of Tuesday, for snow removal and other out of pocket expenses, disregarding damage to property, at $15,000, on a basis of $1,500 a day.

The council opened the discussion of the big storm with a tribute from Mayor George Saxton to "the boys who have done a wonderful job of snow removal."

He added, "I want to thank each disaster council

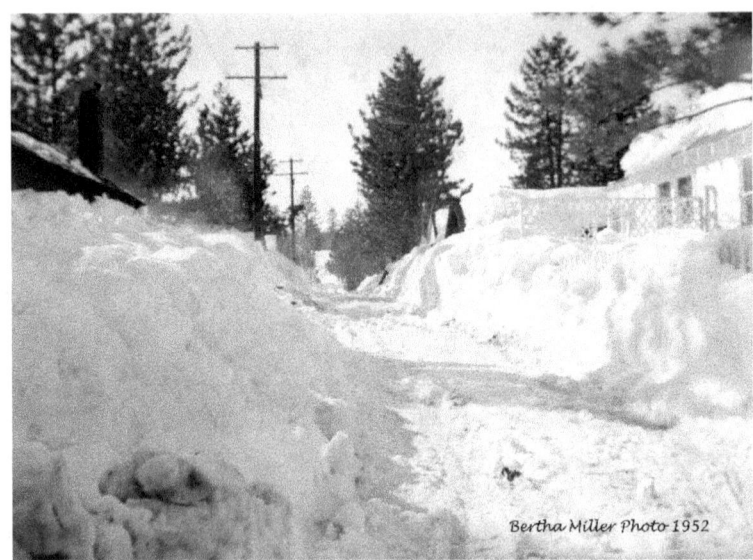
Bertha Miller Photo 1952

head and Rex, for the work you have done. I also would like to extend to Clair Donnenwirth a vote of thanks for the cooperation he has given."

Reihm also praised the many who had worked day and night to meet the requirements of the emergency.

Reihm told the council the emergency orders issued by him were not due to a food shortage, but that the action undoubtedly had saved the collapse of many buildings and snow removal had been organized.

He said the defense council had been assured of help from the governor's office.

Dale Williams, regional coordinator of civilian defense, was quoted as having declared that the defense program is to prevent disaster when possible as well as to meet it.

The possibility of obtaining financial aid from the state was discussed and it was announced that

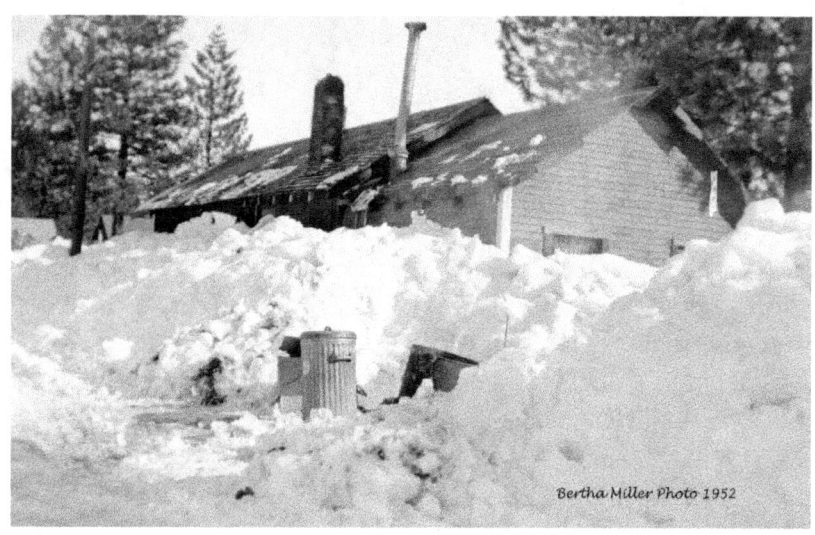
Bertha Miller Photo 1952

Assemblyman Davis planned to introduce legislation for state aid for snow removal in cities as well as in counties.

Reihm said the spirit of cooperation that prevailed was illustrated by the manner in which the oil distributors had worked together pooling supplies and equipment.

Now, he added, we are in a position to give help to the neighboring communities as needed.

Reihm said that if traffic controls were taken off immediately the city would be "right back in the position we were."

Councilman John Richards said he believed the order should be kept in effect and Saxton said, "If we can keep one-way-traffic for trucks and fire equipment we will be lucky."

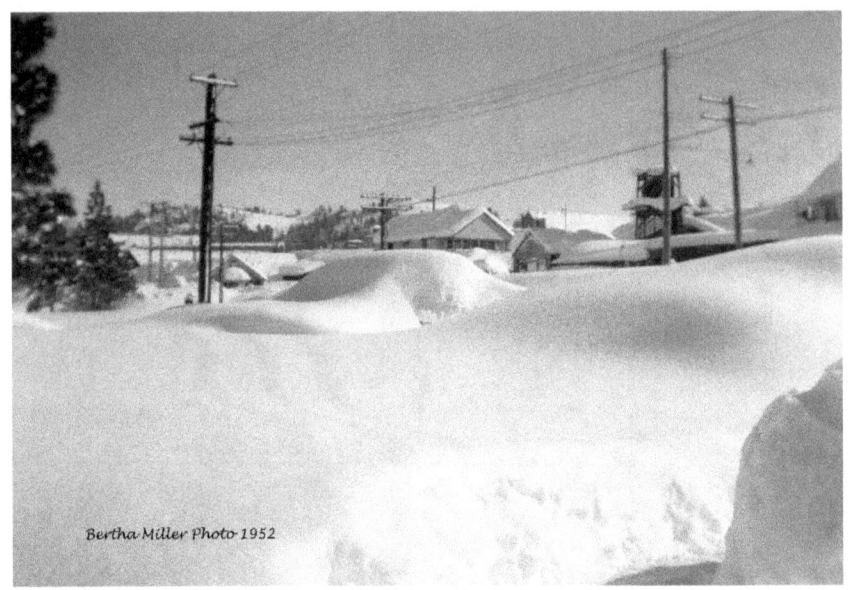
Bertha Miller Photo 1952

The mayor added that if cars were turned loose "We would have congestion in 15 minutes. Each citizen should consider the hazard he would create if he started running around in his car."

All councilmen agreed the order should be kept in effect.

The question of regulating gas installations following last week's fatal explosion also was discussed by the council and Mayor Saxton expressed the view that an ordinance for inspectors should be adopted.

Richards suggested that recommendations be asked from the fire department.

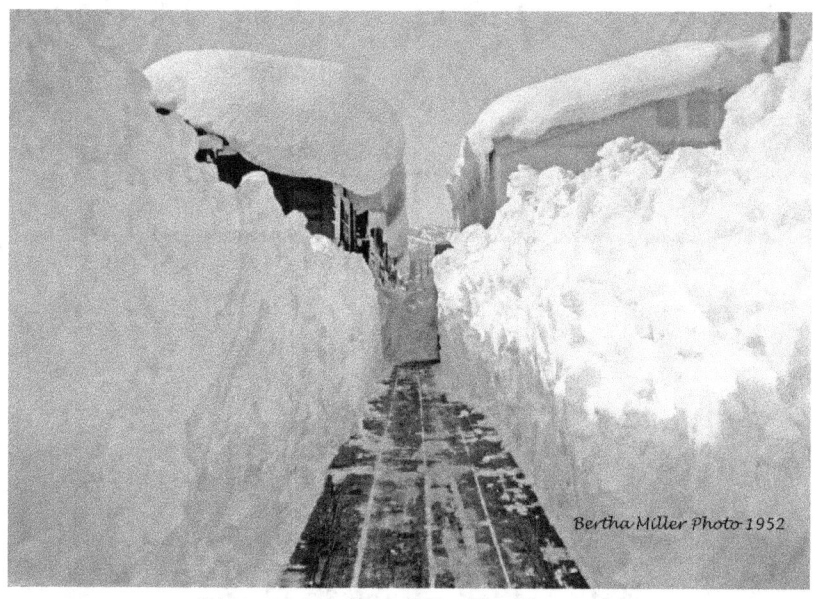

Western Pacific Railroad

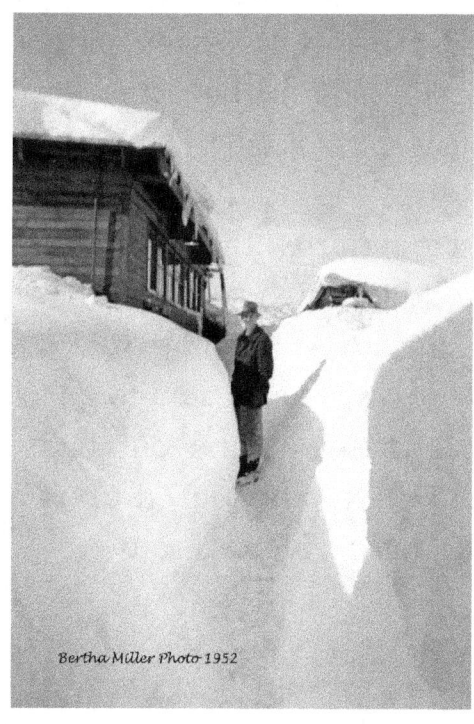

These two photos were taken on January 16th at the WPRR Roundhouse. On the right is my dad, Jack Miller. He shoveled snow at work and again at home—day after day. He was happy when we moved from the mountain town, and never wanted to see snow again.

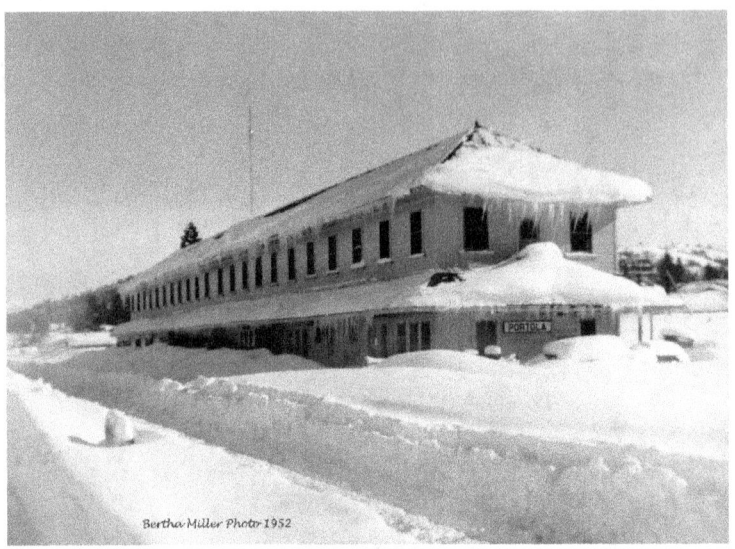
Western Pacific Railroad Depot in Portola

W.P. Getting Back to Normal
Portola Reporter ~ January 24, 1952

Barring unforeseen circumstances, the Western Pacific should be operating on practically a normal basis by tonight (Thursday), according to William Howell, assistant division superintendent.

He reported the canyon route open, and the Bieber-Keddie route was opened Wednesday morning.

Yesterday, a rotary plow was making its way to Reno and is expected to go to Loyalton today.

A diesel engine derailed on the Reno spur was expected to be picked up by a derrick accompanying the rotary, Howell said.

W. P. RAILROAD

Spring at the W. P. Yards. These photos were taken in March 1952.

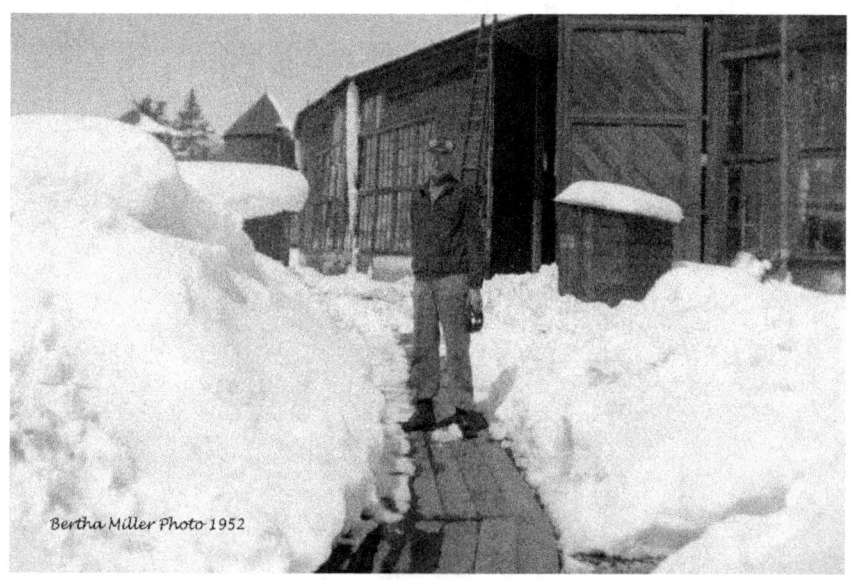

Robert Crumpacker at the roundhouse.

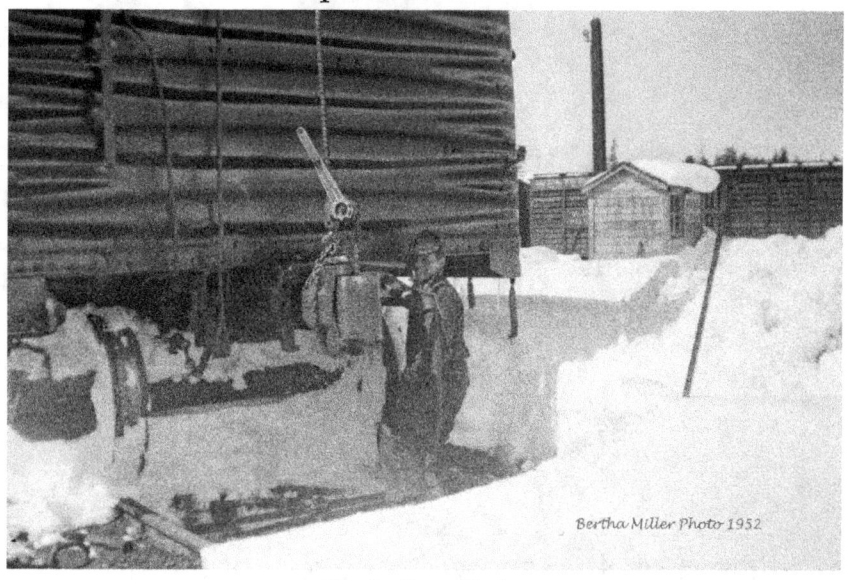

Bob English

W. P. RAILROAD

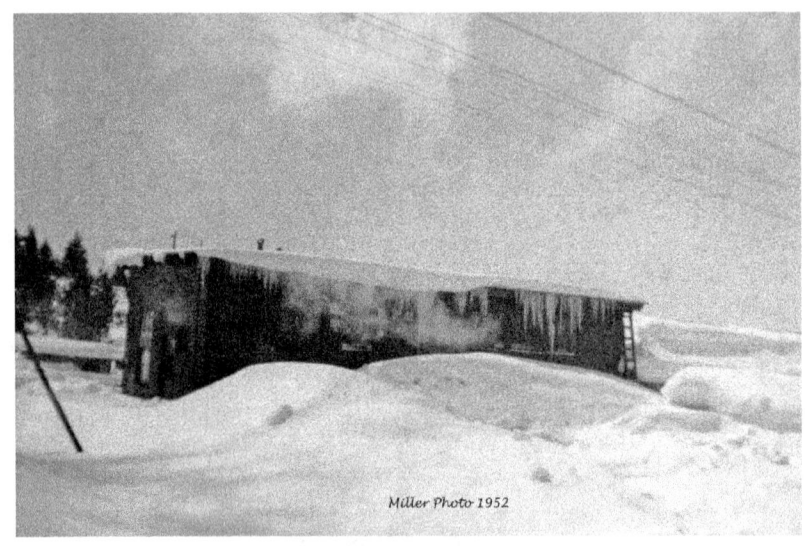

W. P. Store

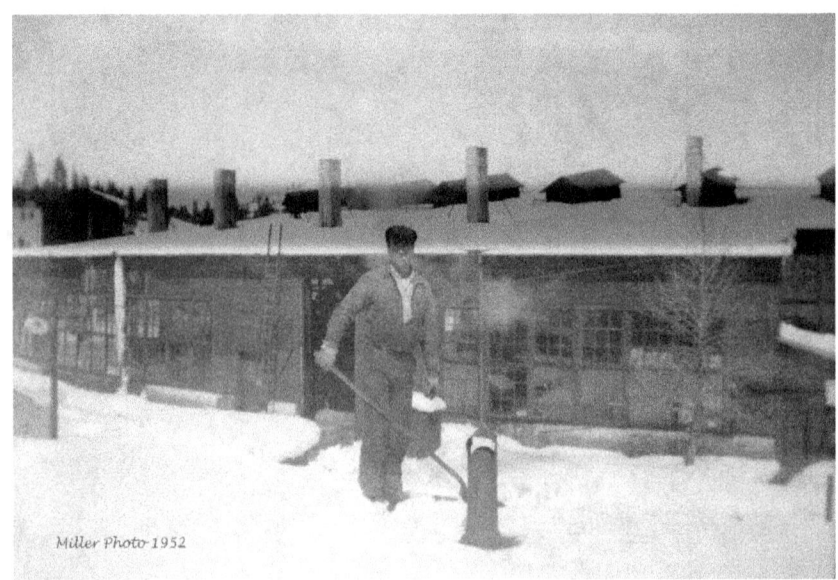

Pate shoveling snow off the roof of the store.

W. P. RAILROAD

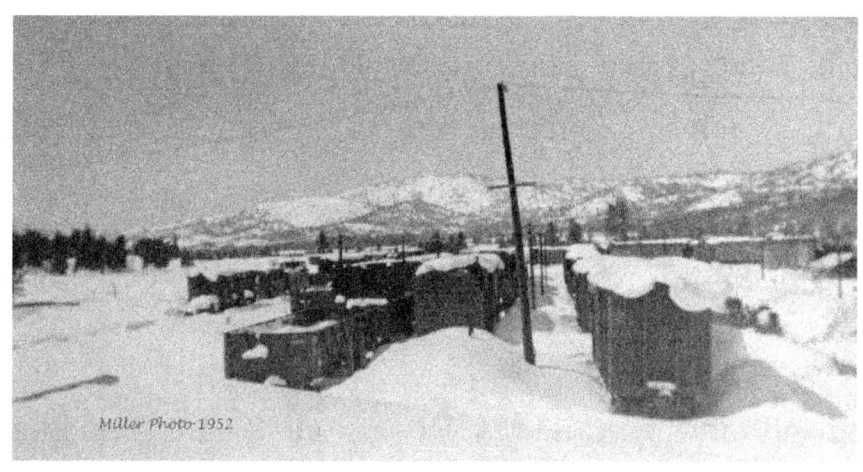

Two photos of the (Repair in Place) RIP track.
March 1952

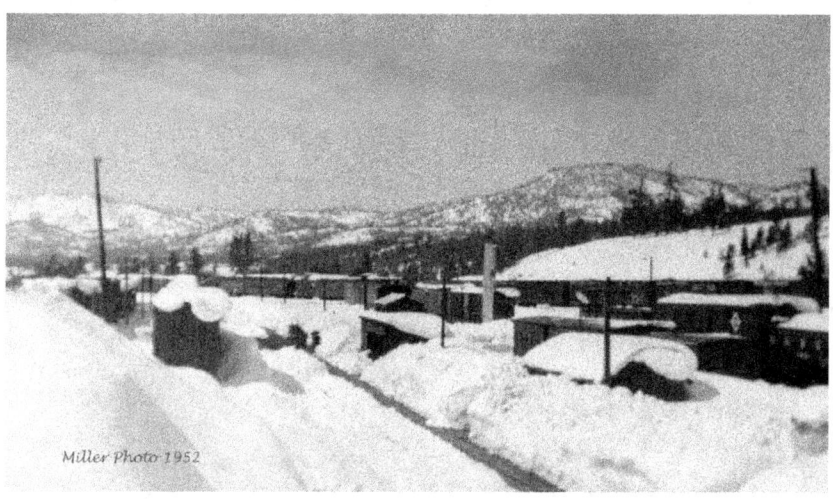

Wrecked Plug Causes Water Shortage

Portola Reporter ~ January 24, 1952

Portola faced an acute water shortage this week when a bulldozer, cutting into a huge drift of show on Nevada Street at the grammar school sheared off a fireplug at a six inch main.

The stream of water washed down the street and drained the reservoir; it was reported by Louis DeArmond, owner of the Portola water company.

Western Pacific pumps assisted in restoring the supply and Wednesday DeArmond expressed hope that a reserve could be built up.

He urged householders to use a minimum of water during this storm crisis.

Markers had been placed at the fire plugs and effort made to dig them out, DeArmond said, but the cut plug either had been overlooked or the marker removed.

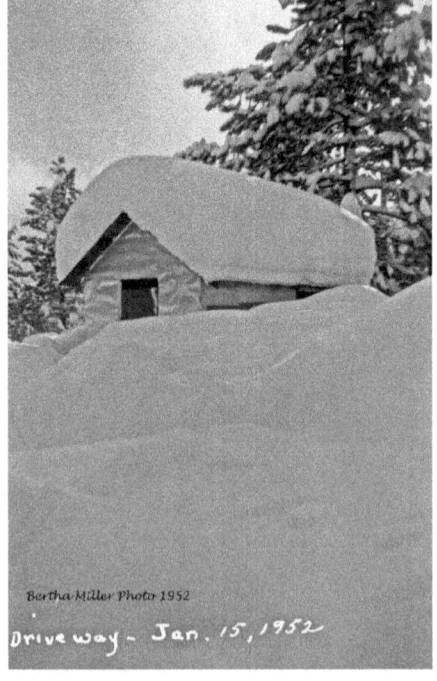

Our driveway
January 15, 1952

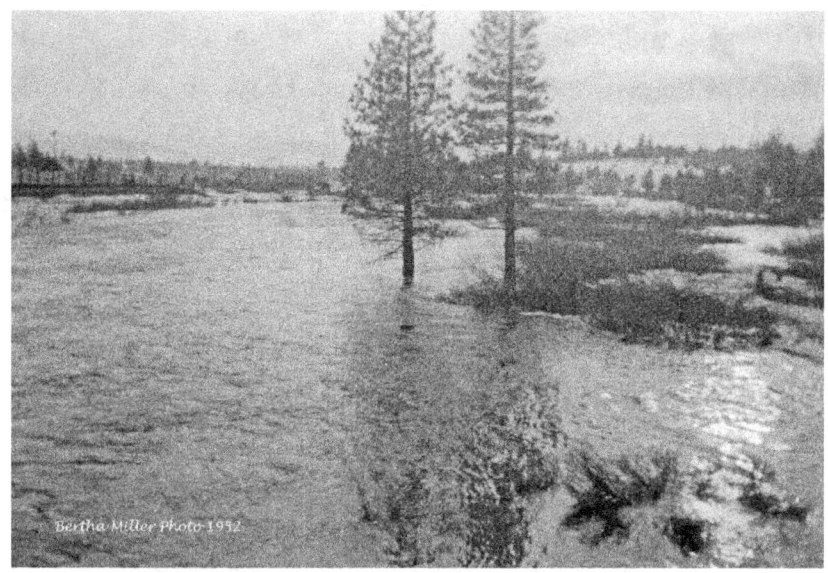

Flooded Feather River April 5, 1952

Thaws Bring Flood Conditions After Big Snow
Unknown Source ~ February 7, 1952

Rain and warm weather that followed the Big Storm brought flood conditions to various sections of eastern Plumas and Sierra Counties at the weekend.

Water got onto the floors of some homes, the basement of Portola Theater was flooded and the fire department was called to assist. The sewage disposal plant also was flooded.

Sewer lines at California and Rio Grande (streets), unable to carry off the water, backed up and a small geyser resulted.

The sewage disposal plant was shut down for a

time, it was announced by George Demery, superintendent; and electric heaters were used to dry out the equipment.

Small rivers ran down many streets, eating gullies into the ice and earth and developing miniature lakes.

Loyalton reports were of 16 inches of water on the main street of the city, and the highway was under water for a distance of three miles Saturday.

Many other sections of the highways in the area were under water and the Feather River Route was badly damaged by the heavy traffic, water and ice.

Cold weather this week retarded the runoff and hopes were held that cold nights and warm days would result in a gradual elimination of flood conditions.

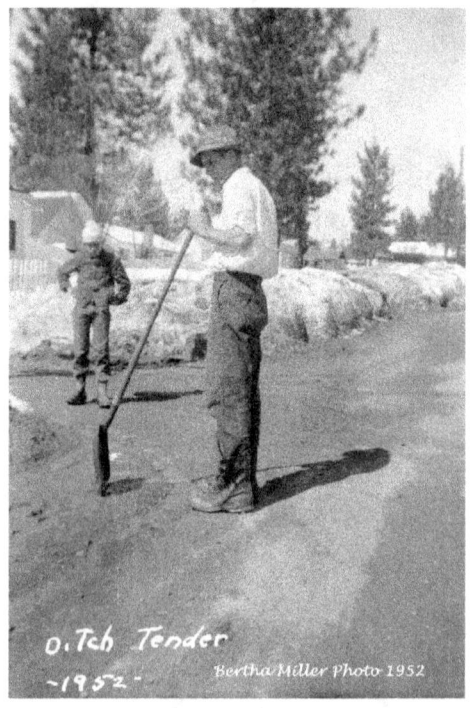

"Ditch tender"
Jack Miller
and son Dennis
April 5, 1952

Spring Flooding

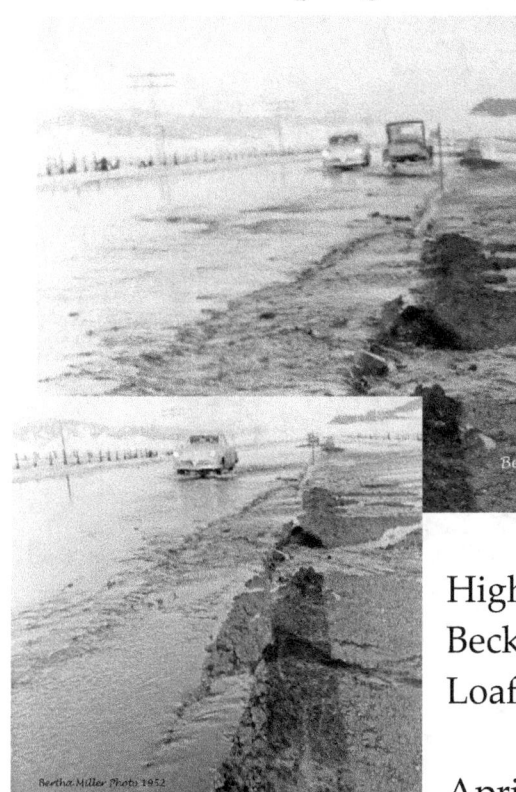

Highway between Beckwourth and Sugar Loaf Mountain

April 6, 1952

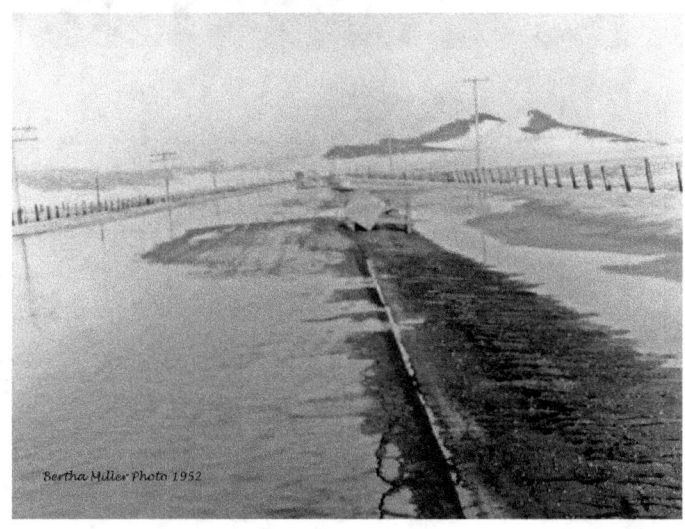

Spring Flooding

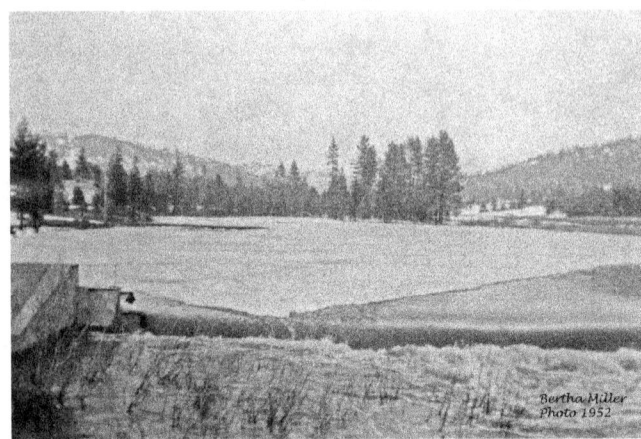

Water over Portola Dam.

April 1952

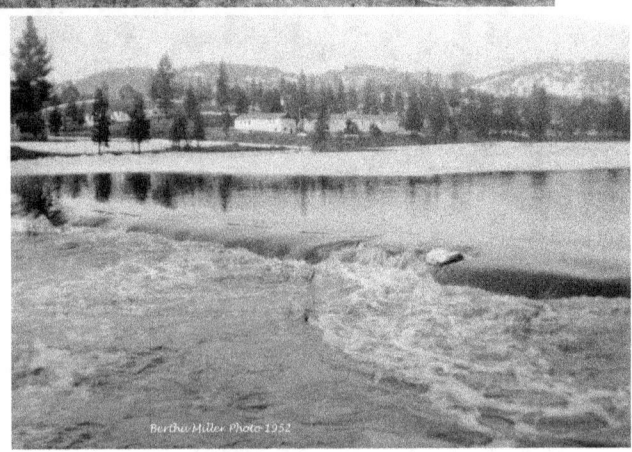

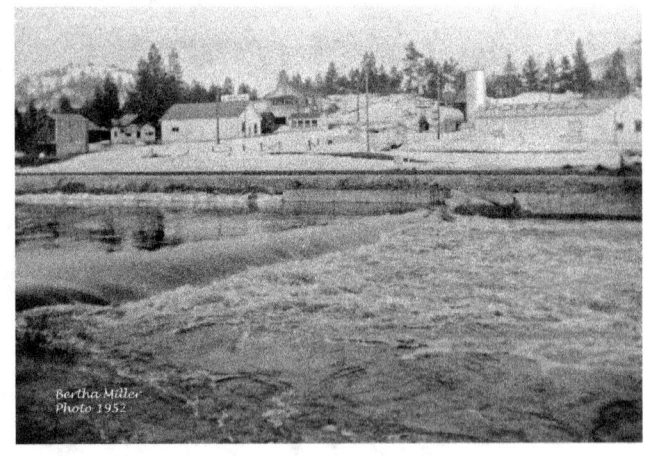

Flood Damage

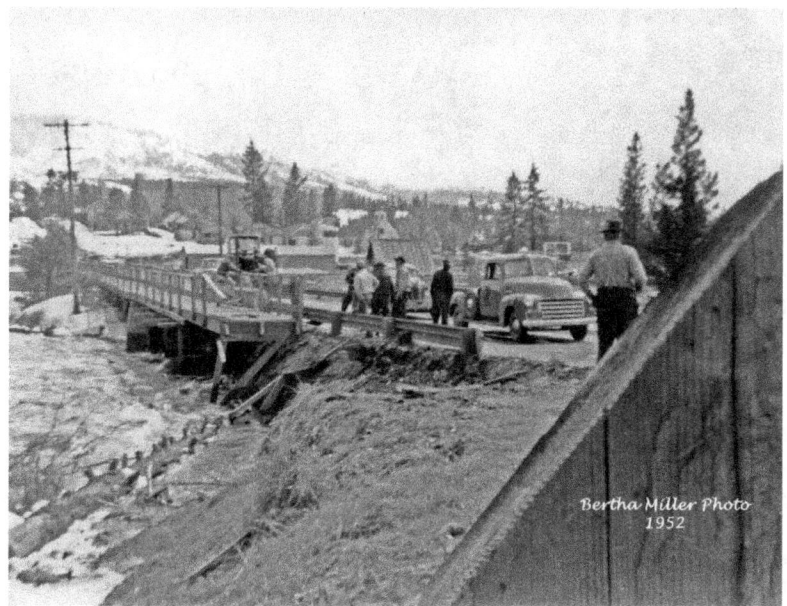

Flood waters threaten bridge. Walkway was collapsed from the heavy snow.– April 1952

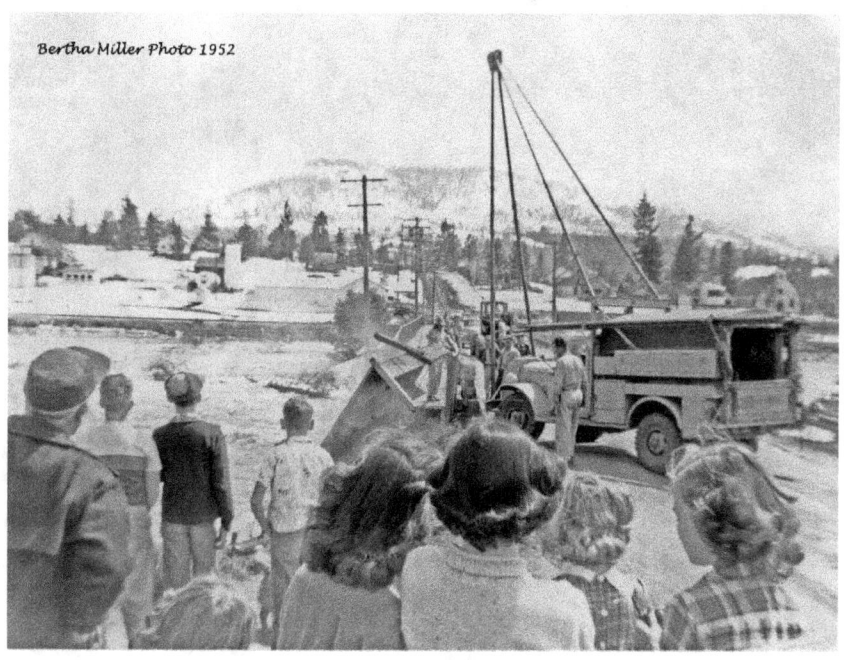

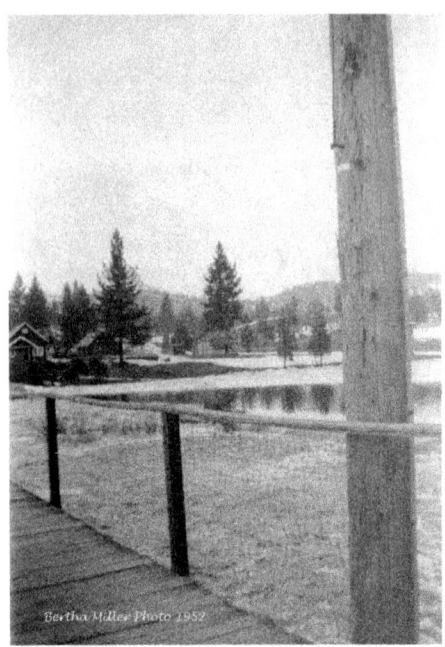

This photo of the wooden walkway that was attached to the bridge was taken from the south side of the river.

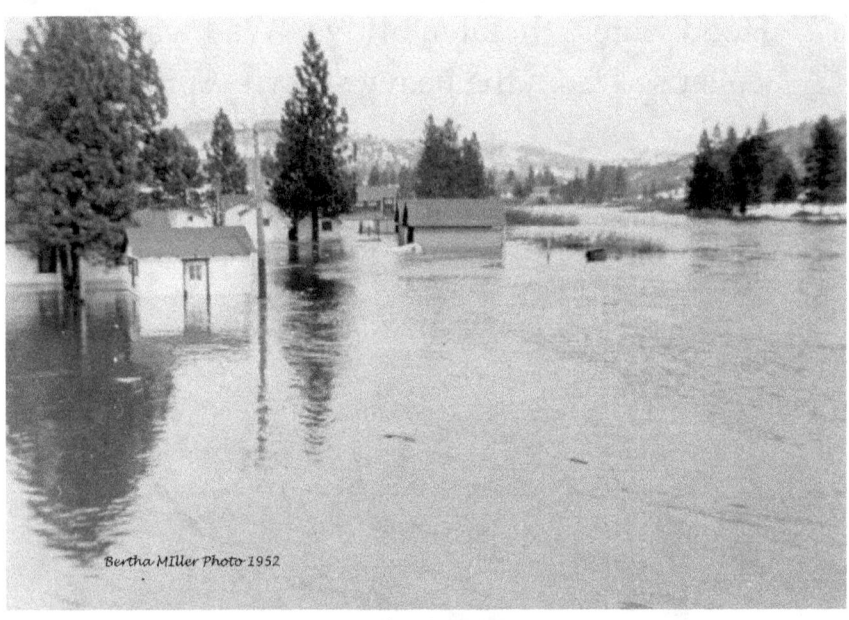

April 6, 1952

AROUND THE AREA

Graeagle Roofs Break Under Snow
January 17 ~ 1952

Weight of the snow crushed the shed over the green chain of the Graeagle Lumber Company plant, and parts of the roof of the box factory and molding mill also caved in.

Snow was about six feet deep on the level, with huge drifts. Some families were reported running low on food Tuesday.

Harley McGuirk and Earl Patterson, driving a rotary plow in an attempt to open the road to Johnsville suffered monoxide gas poisoning when their plow was in a huge snow ditch and the fumes came into the cabin. Their condition was reported all right Tuesday.

Members of the B. G. Vernozzi family narrowly escaped injury when a rotary snow plow hurled a huge chunk of ice through the front window with terrific force. Mac Perazzi had warned the family away from the window a second before.

Vinton: 'Worst Storm Since 1890'
January 17, 1952

Roy Robinson of Vinton reported "just a lot of

snow" when asked how the Sierra Valley was surviving the big storm.

He reported six feet at the highway corner to Loyalton and huge drifts.

Ranchers, he said, were experiencing considerable trouble in feeding their cattle.

Robinson quoted Rudolph Ramelli, Sierra Valley historian, as declaring the storm was the worst since 1890.

Beckwourth Says Biscuits Good
January 17, 1952 ~ Portola Reporter

Beckwourth, hoping that snow plows would reach there Wednesday night, survived the storm in good shape, with plenty of food and most people eating biscuits in the absence of bread, it was reported by Mrs. Louise Ghidossi.

A shortage of fuel was threatened, she said.

Loyalton Reports O.K. in storm
January 17, 1952 ~ Portola Reporter

Loyalton came through this much of the big storm in fine shape, it was reported by Ed White.

He expressed hope that the road to Vinton would be open today (Thursday).

Part of the two lumber sheds and part of the dry shed of the Clover Valley Lumber Company collapsed under the snow.

Oil to Loyalton
January 24, 1952 ~ Unknown source

Portola oil distributors went into Loyalton yesterday to make deliveries and relieve an acute fuel situation in the Sierra Valley city.

The town also was reported low on fresh foods, but no suffering was reported and the streets were being fairly well opened.

Traffic on the streets was limited to emergencies with a pile of snow eight feet high in the center of Main Street.

Increasing Sierra Snowfall Deals Death, Stops All Travel, Inflicts Damage
January 15, 1952 ~ Sacramento Bee

Susanville is Isolated

Susanville, Lassen County . . . is isolated by the heaviest snowstorm in 30 years. The snow depth in the city is ranging from 5 to 6 feet. Ranchers have been affected, being unable to get feed to their stock. Schools in Susanville and Honey Lake Valley are closed throughout tomorrow. Snowplows have been unable to cope with the heavy drifts. One snowplow operator on Highway 36 between Susanville and Westwood, Lassen County, has not been heard from since Monday night. Business houses closed yesterday and the owners diverted their activities to shoveling snow from their roofs.

Wildlife Drama in Sierra Valley
Portola Reporter ~ January 24, 1952

Sierra Valley survived the Big Storm in good shape with no losses of cattle, according to Mrs. Frank Dotta. REA power service was restored Sunday evening and it was possible to pump water for cattle that were beginning to suffer from lack of water.

Jack rabbits of the area were hard hit, however.

She could look from the ranch window and see coyotes ditching them. Many others died as a direct result of the storm.

Hundreds of the animals collected in the ranch corrals and areas were "black with them."

As the storm continued, she said, the numbers apparently diminished by half. During the recent years the rabbit had been increasing greatly.

Mrs. Dotta said that Charles Trossi had skied out from his ranch, a distance of 3 miles on old long boards and had reported seeing numerous deer, but none of them dead.

Alton Young, Quincy, county farm advisor, was in the valley assisting ranchers care for their stock.

Plans Made to Feed County Deer
Portola Reporter ~ January 24, 1952

Plans for feeding deer in eastern Plumas County were being made this week.

A call for volunteers and equipment to be used as

soon as weather permits was issued by Game Warden George Shockley and it was tentatively proposed to have volunteers cut cedar bows for food.

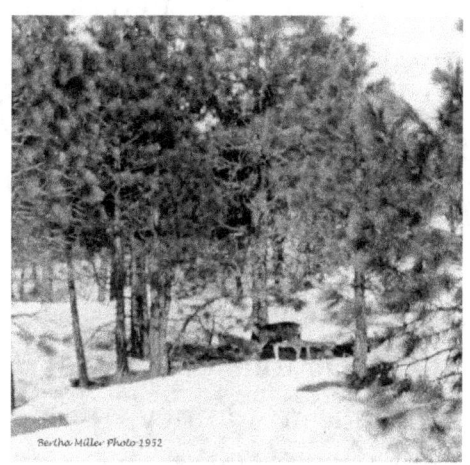

Deer in April 1952

In addition Jack Farnsworth, president of the county conservation league had a supply of grain and salt for distribution.

The grain and salt were provided by the county board of supervisors.

Shockley said that while the benefits of feeding were questionable, "if it is possible, to relieve the situation we will."

He asked for volunteers and those having equipment notify Lloyd E. Boone, justice of the peace and member of the county fish and game commission at 137-w or 194.

Pickup trucks, snow shoes and hatchets are needed, he said.

Sidelights of the Storm
Portola Reporter ~ January 24, 1952

January snowfall, according to the Plumas National Forest records, accounted for 13.05 inches of water, bringing the total seasonal precipitation for central Plumas County to 42.04 inches as of January 21. Daily measurements of snowfall in Quincy recorded a total of 75 inches of snow to date.

* * *

The Plumas National Forest headquarters in Quincy estimated 1190 tons of snow shoveled off the roofs of the buildings in Quincy, representing more than 400,000 gallons of water. Some Portola boys claim to have shoveled more than that off one roof.

* * *

Thirty-five feet of the footbridge across the Feather River in Portola, collapsed Sunday morning under the weight of the snow.

* * *

The regional office of the civil defense council arranged for 200 shovels to be sent from the forest service office in Susanville to Portola for emergency use.

* * *

Portola made television during the Big Storm. Telephone calls from Los Angeles reported views of the city, taken from an airplane, were televised.

COMMENTS ABOUT THE SNOW

On Top of the World
January 17, 1952 ~ Portola Reporter
(Weekly newspaper column)

Peering over a snow bank

* * *

Portolans pretty much showed pioneer spirit during the storm.

* * *

They helped each other and they helped strangers who were stranded in the midst.

* * *

When the Greyhound lines failed to care for the passengers, who were in the stalled busses, many Portola families took passengers into their homes.

* * *

It is quite a contrast to the story told by Herb Caen, San Francisco columnist.

Said Herby:

"Up in the Sierra snow country they're talking (nastily) about this . . . Happened during the N'Years weekend storms, when the highway was suddenly closed to traffic. Dozens of stranded motorists, truck drivers, service men, etc. battled their way to a nearby, widely-known lodge—where they spent hours (and plenty of money) buying dinner and drinks . . . Suddenly at 2 a.m. the manager announced:

"We're locking up the place. Everybody that doesn't have a room reservation will have to get out.

"The moans and pleas ('just let us sit in the lobby') didn't do any good. Out into the black storm trudged the homeless ones, many of them with children. And they spent the rest of the night in their stalled cars, with the motors running for warmth—risking carbon monoxide poisoning in preference of freezing to death.

"There are some wonderful people up in the snow country. But the owner of that lodge isn't one of them."

* * *

We agree with Herb, there are wonderful people in the snow country.

* * *

Guys like that resort owner are scarce, thank goodness.

* * *

And here's a cheer for the girls who manned the telephone company switchboard during the storm.

* * *

A lot of people, apparently, didn't have anything to do but sit around and call their neighbors and chatter.

* * *

Others had to make business calls, and there were abnormal numbers of long distance calls that were necessary.

* * *

The result was that the switchboard was flooded for days at a time and the girls worked like crazy to handle the load.

* * *

And they had to operate that outmoded, obsolete, antiquated equipment for which the Bell Company make a charge—and constantly want to increase the rates.

* * *

And another cheer for the city and county road crews, and Supervisor Donnenwirth, the T.W.J. Company of Deleker and its men, Rex Reihm and the power company crew, and a lot of others for the battle they put up in a desperate effort to keep the city and county from begging completely.

--sb

(Stan Bailey ?)

The Reporter too had inconveniences in the big storm. This issue isn't all that is desired, but—

There are many duties to perform, the telephone lines were bogged down, there was disaster council work to do, and then the paper.

Other C. L. Neely books you may enjoy…

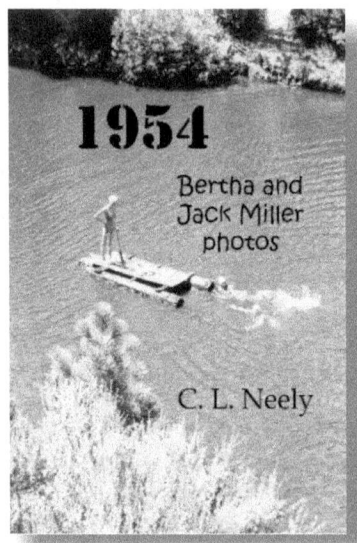
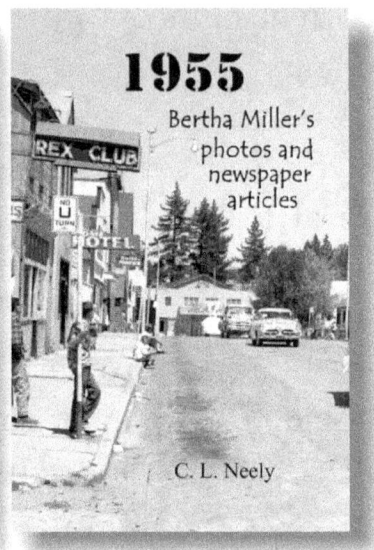
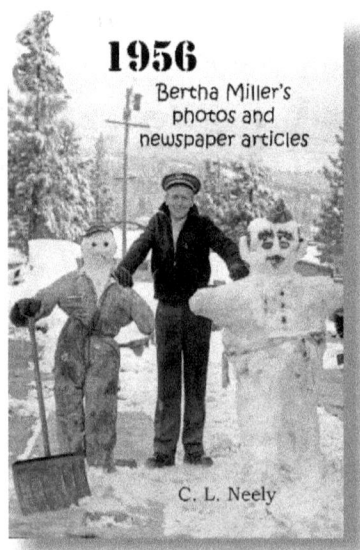
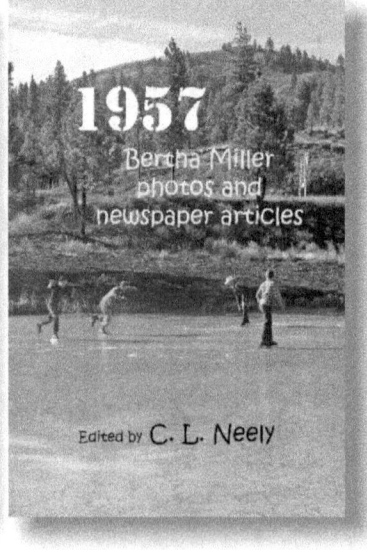

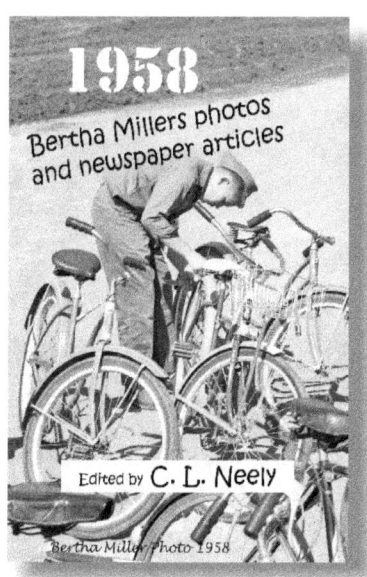
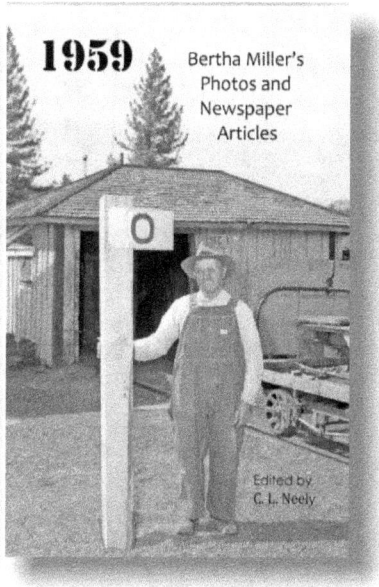
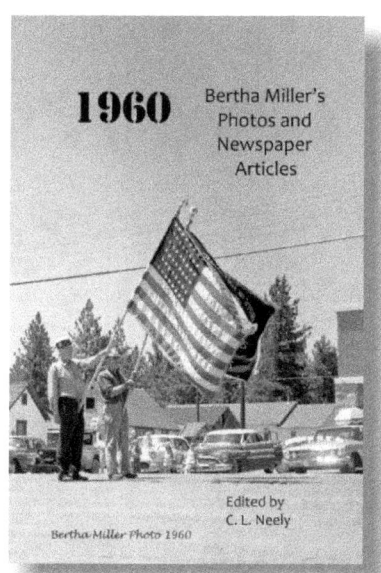
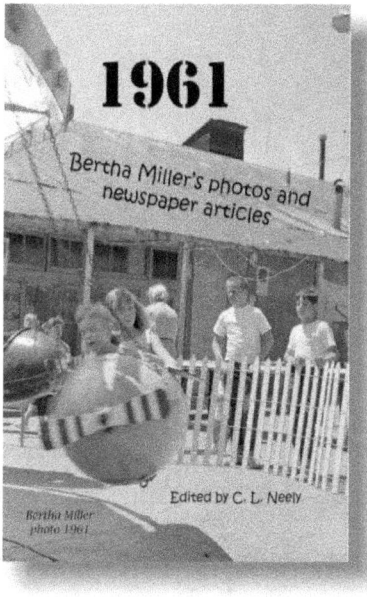

www.ingramcontent.com/pod-product-compliance
Lightning Source LLC
Chambersburg PA
CBHW050023230526
45470CB00003B/1107